LIFE, AS IT APPEARS

Leif Robertsson

LIFE, AS IT APPEARS

Cover: Leif Robertsson
Förlag: BoD · Books on Demand, Östermalmstorg 1, 114 42 Stockholm, bod@bod.se

Tryck: Libri Plureos GmbH, Friedensallee 273, 22763 Hamburg, Tyskland

ISBN: 978-91-8097-038-9

In the gloomy forest
lives a sick god.
In the dark forest the flowers are so pale
and the birds so shy.
Why is the wind full of warning whispers
and the road dark with gloomy forebodings?
In the shadow lies the sick god
and dreams evil dreams...

Edit Södergran

(translated from Swedish with Google translate)

*

Trying to achieve
some wisdom
for my mind's comfort,
soft as the moon’s reflection
over darkening waters.

Among the market traders,
I seek the fruit from
the tree of knowledge.
Sourly sweet, red and true.

With increasing amount
of trickling saliva,
I sing the praise of learning.
Knowledge burdens
only those who lack it.

*

The invitation
makes me nervous.
Eel eating parties
aren't my thing.
Trying to fit in.
It's not going so well.
I would have rather
stayed by the water.

A rowboat split
the water surface
with silent oars.
The pike-perch
glared sourly
in the reeds
and youngsters
sat on the shore
shyly flirting.

I didn't get to see
all of this.
My eyes were

completely empty.
No tears.
Just the empty
flower of longing.

*

Just heard from
infinity.
Laika is no longer alive.
Maybe I should take a
course or do
some time travels.

Is it so or so?
So much misery.
So much destruction.
So much to do.

A gift from nowhere.
Neither paper nor strings.
The song sounds
like something
from the abandoned.

Discord from broken
devices.
I no longer remember
the lunar lander.

*

Traces a longing.
A longing
long longed for.
For generations.
Maybe one day
a moment will
become real.
Surprising in an
astonished dawn.
A hint, a glimpse in
a sparkling suit.

All the senses
make themselves
known.
Feel, see and hear
everything in a
constant storm
and how it tastes
and smells of
earth and fire.

As we long

*

Selected thoughts,
carefully carved
out of consciousness,
age in old
stained envelopes.
As.
The echo of silence
was the most precious
thing we inherited.

Between our fingers
small pieces of our lives
drip while images
of our most secret
thoughts
are gathered in
small baskets
of the finest filigree.
Well preserved
out of reach
for the future.

*

Over the instrument's
black ebony,
a forsaken
sparrow chirps,
its wings
no longer carrying
its own worries.
Accompanied by
its brittle shadow,
it meets its reflection
in pretended joy.

Evocative noises
fill the void
after the plumage's
unexpected flight.
A luminous
shimmer lingers
for the remainder
of the day.
Millisecond
by millisecond,
eternity strives

towards
its unattainable
completion.

*

Overgrown
with old memories.
A swarm,
a living mass.
A lump that suffocates.
The hardest,
the almost forgotten
emerges from
the depths
of many fathoms.
Detaches and clings.
The dust of regret
blackens the features
and the mask,
with its dim gaze,
invites.

Blinded by
the blue lightning.
A silent echo
of the child's
concern.
They swarm

no more.
They warn of
fire,
of flooded
fields.
Storms over
defenseless
innocence.
The child
of anxiety float
downstream.

*

In the light from
the empty face
of the canvas,
a myrtle sprig
on an annealed
table top.
A survival strategy
behind closed blinds.
Anemia,
bread shortage,
iciness.
The motif
fails to appear.
The oil thickens
and the brushes
lose their hair.
Empty canvases
piles up.

The splendor
of the meadows
shrinks to a naked
nothingness.

Freedoms
are curtailed
in the name of
the defense of freedom.

Desperately paints
a new vision
in anger.
Traffic thickens
behind the glued
activists.
The wings of
music takes off.
I call out a toast
for hope.
Maybe …
Must …
Must not fall.
Not …
Not sink into
the swamp of doubt.

*

I buy a ticket to
an unknown place.
When the journey
begins, a slight euphoria
sets in,
a feeling
like that of a
good fishing luck.
Blinded by the view.
Dazed and
naked before
the truth-tellers.

Strolling through
the remade city park.
New fountains.
The band rounds
the aviary with
pounding drums
and roaring trumpets.
The cockatoos
crouch under
the mesh screens.

Don’t feed the animals.
Don’t bathe in the pond.
Don’t eat in the bus.
Don’t fall asleep
behind the wheel.

At dusk
the jackdaws
land in the treetops
of the esplanade.
Chattering.
Citizens drag
grocery bags
and homework.
The soccer stadium
is deserted and empty.
Reports of terror
and war.

*

In Kristinehamn
and New York
the sparrow-hawk
flies on light wings.
Heyerdahl sailed
a reed boat
across the sea.

In the gentle,
salt-saturated breeze
of the autumn darkness,
we feel a longing.
A yearning for the sea
and the skies.
Rushing, swishing.
Falling and rising
forward on an
uncharted flight.

Purposeful,
improvised and
unthought-out,

at cruising speed
through life's
amusement park.

*

Between now and
the next episode.
Before, after
and right now.

A manhood in
the meaningless
infinity.
Only the hare cares.
Understands
the value of listening.

Tomorrow
all the verses
will be retold,
the written ones
as well as the ones
only thought of.

In the narrative,
traces of sorrow
are mixed with
the cirrus clouds
of the summer sky.

*

What we rarely see,
the hidden and the forgotten.
The new time is pulling
in a different direction.

Sometimes something
is perceived,
something faintly
familiar.
Capillary force lifts
the anxiety
up to eye level.

We stop.
Look around.
Listen for
faint breaths
from what
we call life.
We hear
the whales' song
about the
sadden sea.

Through
the hysterical
funfair shout,
we hear
the people's lament.
We press our palms
over our ears
and close our eyelids.

*

Snow drifts
over the locked out
gloomy days.

While the key of grace
dreams of
milk and ginger,
the ice melts
under the horse's
slippery hooves.
While
the last episode
of the first season
rolls out.

The glowed insides
of history
houses the dead fire.
Meanwhile
the used
acanthus leaves
fall.

*

The expansion
of the universe
widens
the limit
of its finitude.
Thus, time stretches
the span of our lives.
The butterflies at Haga
mingle about chaos
in dynamic systems.
There's a storm
in Kashmar
where the flame
of the cypress
burns a hole
in the sky.

A conic section
of time seeks
to move the limit
of the possible.
The world,

a system that
lives by itself.
We will never
live a dignified life
on Mars.

Zarathustra planted
the cypress.

*

Terminals and
stations.
Signals that
accuse.

Institutions and
establishments.
With self-swinging
doors.
Pendulum movements.

The light in the end
of the tunnel
flickers and beckons.
Out. Out of.
Out into the late
longing of the afternoon.

The sea smoke dances
over the morning waters,
where my being
travels by.

*

Clenching my fists
in the black hole
of reflection.
The hourglass is colored
in autumn sandstone.
Turning the hour,
waiting for sadness.
Olive blossoms
over the cemetery wall.
All the dead children.

Signed agreements
are scattered by the wind.
Departing east and west.
Confronts all these images.
The unpleasant eye candy
leaves no peace.
The guardian of all scents
searches in his memory
banks for rosewater
and compassion.

*

In a sweaty
feverish dizziness,
man trembles
as if in a trance.
The budding
is met by
a resistance,
a restrained
minor chord.

Then the train
leaves,
the grey train
that is expected
to arrive at
the platform
when time sings
ballads.

It is in
times of waiting
that they usually
take off.

Floats like a fog.
Meaningful
little things
collect in the
corners.
The treetops
decrowns
and the foghorns
whistle.
As October
moves towards
reluctant completion,
time changes foot.
Outside, the search
continues.

*

The spear thrower
looks for the prey.
Wants to know
where it hit.
Chews idly
on a broken twig
while Cassiopeia
sails towards eternity.

The wormwood
of success
stings deeply.
The quill pen
quivers, longing
for the unwritten
pages.

Trembling a little
in the morning meeting.
The meeting
with the manhood
that ravages
the world.

*

Slightly nauseous,
she laid her head
on a soft tuft
of green moss.
Thoughts about
everything elusive
that constantly
moved in her world
were still swarming
around her tender brain
at this moment.
An insight landed
on her like the first
butterfly of spring
on a not-yet-blooming
crocus.
Black holes don't
only exist
in the remotest
hiding places
of the cosmos,
she thought.
Every one of us

are born with
two small black holes
that devour all light
that is directed at them.
No light escapes.
Once it has passed
the event horizon,
the light enters
the center of thought
where all the collected
information shapes
the creative process
that is man.

*

The excessive rain
puts all the fish
to sleep.
The gray fog,
a blanket of lead.

In the galaxy,
messages are sent
in the finest fonts
of light.
A breather
on the road.
A fool's defense.
Excuses are
collected in a row.

Outside,
the pollen irritates
the mucous membranes.
The twang of bronze
disturbs the sleep
and in the right-wing
jungle the elephants

are dancing.
The salt doesn't
get any saltier.

*

When the blackness
of night is heavy,
the light slowly
wakes up,
rises and walks
towards a new day.
Helpless but determined,
dawn seeks a path
towards the forest's edge,
making its way
between frozen trunks.

The hare gets stuck
in a crack in the light.
A shadow cast
among other shadows.
Seeking meaning
where there is none.
A fallen tree leads
the path past itself.

They fall when
the wind is strong.

The light, however,
is there.
It gives hope
to our dejection.

The little stream
awakens
from its slumber,
shakes a little
and sets off towards
the wide embrace
of the sea.
Mixes with
other fresh streams.
Thus, the day
fills the leaky vessel
of time in defiance
of human folly.

*

We sleep sweetly
in this strange reality
where the world
is torn in pieces.
We agonize.
Don't know how
it's all going to be.
We sleep sweetly
and refuse to see
what we are doing
wrong.
Somebody else,
we think.

*

The tuning fork
vibrates at 440 Hz.
The cilia swing
along in the same a.
Time slows down
and the low flame
trembles.

The cattle huddle
in the pointed shadow
of the pyramid,
and on the Gulf of Riga,
white sails chase
a ripple on the surface.
The fields sound
of bird's twitter
while derogatory words
are spoken in hidden worlds.
Horse dung remains
on the promenade
until it has become
one with the universe.

Here but no more,
scream the signs loudly.
The roaches and the ants
play hide and seek
with Mr. Chanterelle.
The lord of the flies
doesn't seem to care much.
The model stands
in contrapposto
and thinks about life,
as it appears.

*

With flushing cheeks
and frozen smiles,
my little friends
climb purposefully
towards the top.
The citizens listen wearily
to the young poet's sweaty
reading on human
shortcomings.
The Big Dipper
trudges along
on its endless path
while the hypnotist
lulls the audience to sleep.
An illusion of a
spectacle appears.

A warm welcome
to today's poetry.
Summer winds outside.
The radio announcer,
wearing his most
dazzling smile,

thinks about his
latest investment.
The chaos theory
casts its shadow
over parliamentary work
while the cosmic
background radiation
celebrates its birthday.
Wrapped in meaningless
small talk, delicious
homemade theories
are on offer.

Before anyone knows,
the climate has delivered
one and a half degrees
and a tv channel has sent
the final part of
a hopeless celebrity contest.
A stunning green
adorns the recently
bare branches.
Tuesday meetings drag on
and the final nuclear waste
disposal has major
space problems
while the parking attendant

pulls his weight.
However, the sing-along
never seems to be
affected by the outside
world.

The ants on the ground,
on the slippery,
silvery surface of the rocks,
are hardly bothered
by the investigator's
final report.
Half-conscious,
the exhausted
deliverer of mail
brings another
advertising insert.
In the auditorium,
the boys' choir
performs one of many
lust-murdered versions of
"Bridge over Troubled Water"
while the reactor contributes
a few more kilos of spent fuel.

The principal, for his part,
is forced to report

any student suspected
of being inappropriately
educated.
Mile after mile
of deep forests
sweep by outside the
compartment windows
while greed starts war
in another part of
the world.
The yellow-brown
autumn falls softly
to the ground,
rotten for the benefit
and joy of the earth.

*

The weeping silent day
seeks its answers
in revealing and
sympathetic verses.
Never more
lonely solitude,
as square-angled
as in the evening.
Inboard, run over
and choleric,
the sleepwalking
pathfinder commits
a kind of imperceptible
hara-kiri.

Thus, spoke the versatile
and moonstruck mystic
of his supposed experiences.
Of the rower who
carried his worn oars
on wounded shoulders
as a torture instrument.
An early sign of madness.

As if higher powers
were playing along
in imaginary charades.

Under a heavy
lead blanket,
a long-faded image
of fear is evoked.
The fear that can be
traced in every reed
and straw that bends
in the wind.
Seeking strength
in the blissful repeats
heard from the beginning
of eternity.

*

Behind the seventh
locked door,
morning, day,
and evening
already dwell.

The fifth door opens
towards the great
wealth of light.
Meets her love.

When, as the night,
she unites with those
already departed,
the castle turns
into darkness again.

The key that opens
the heart's gate
spreads the voice
of light over the world.

*

Swimming in deep water.
Slow smooth strokes.
Like flying high in the sky
but in water. A hundred meters
down to solid ground.
Losing speed and falling,
falling through air or water.
Dying any way.

Striding through life
at will. Sometimes
an easy slide,
sometimes a rough ride
over rugged rocks.
Gradually losing
the steering ability
and falling. Falling.
Falling through
wordless sludge.

Perhaps never
finding myself again.

*

Thoughts run
in uncharted terrain.
Everything echoes
of the barbarity
of our time.
Is there any light
in the darkness?

The zeitgeist
mercilessly push
down our fragile
souls deeply
into the cold
womb of despair.

A gap opens in the gray
and we squeeze our way
towards hope.
Must try.
There must be
a life to live
for the unborn.

*

The attentive reader
reads between the lines
about wounds
that heal slowly.
The message's
tension points
leave traces
that sting deeply.
The clown's eyes
no longer cry.
Not even when
the thorns of the words
pierce deep into the soul.

Dawn breaks forth
from his chest, blackened
by the dust clouds
of the detonations.
One day, one night
flees into oblivion.
Ravage there
and creates
inexplicable anxiety.

*

Silvery serpentines
flow down the smooth
sides of the clouds
and are quickly
swallowed up
by the plowed
gray scale of the earth.
Empty hearts take
the remote-controlled
escalator up to the top floor
to meet the guru
of supreme happiness.
When payment has been made,
the annoying cramps disappear
in the direction of the tangent.
However, only temporarily.
A transient state
of happiness
in the late hours
of euphoria.
The hangover
creeps in when the joy
of buying has ebbed

and the seller
asks for your rating
of the payment process.

*

Like a self-playing
piano in the morning …
The night had been
eventful, more so
than expected.
My thoughts played
in all musical parts.
Sang with many voices.
Like a self-playing
piano from evening
to morning.

The dreams had
unified me with
the most vulnerable.
The degraded,
dehumanized, killed.
The raped and
the dumped. Extradited.
The nightmares
made me understand
the meaninglessness
of suffering.

*

As the morning mists
clear, the light-shy figures
retrace into their musty holes.
There, others await reports
from the night's unsettlement.
What has happened
at the front?
How many innocents
have been killed?
How much land
and property
has been laid to waste?
Have we mutilated,
destroyed, and then
glorified our desire
for revenge?

As the morning mists
clear, we turn our empty
eyes away.
We refuse to see the ravaged
land and the amputated
orphaned children.

Cannot bear to hear
grown men and women
cry out their bottomless
despair over their
tattered offspring.
We have only
defended ourselves.

As the morning mists
clear, we thank our allies
who silently observe
or turn their gaze inward
in their cowardly refusal
to defend human rights.
We gratefully receive
new weapon systems,
still warm from the factories,
that generates fat profits
for shareholders far away.
Men with greedily
stretched out hands
from white, starched cuffs
without the slightest
stain of gunpowder.

*

Ice-bird over
frozen sea.
Sad voices from
brittle throats.
Ice-bird sings
in the flight.

The winter storm
sweeps over the bare
frozen ground.
The chimneys smoke
hesitates and falls
silent.
Rests in dormancy.

Under the roof ridges,
a longing smolder.
An expectation.
The sadness
spreads across
the continents.
Drawn-out cries
from frightened

young birds.
The wings flapping
roars over the devastated
landscape.
The jet stream writes
with a quill about
the state of the earth.
Flows swiftly
through the atmosphere.

Emotions rush through
the bloodstream,
frost-bitten premonitions
of the future.
The heart knows
the Ice-bird's flight.
Follows the tracks
of the wings
towards the end.

*

The absent conversations.
The introverted features.
Skipped necessities.
Where were you
in your dream last night?
Heartfelt desire to hear
your innermost thoughts,
wrapped in rustling
cellophane that leads
them towards some
kind of completion.

The memory games
roll on over overturned
sense of self.
A trapped plague.
Stomach aches
and migraines.
A walk on the dream's
wandering paths
might offer some relief.
Or a visit from
rustling wings.

Overlooks all
transgressions.
I've heard that
you have
a really nice
view here.
Reaches
all the way
to the red horizon.
Eyes tear up
and distrust
grows with every
missed turn.
The trees shed
their truths.

Workshops whizzes
across the sky.
It’s certainly possible
to repair broken
promises.
An intuitive
interface may turn
everything back
on to its right track.
The sea rises
over all hearts.

Salty and reinforced
the day strives towards
that horizon.
The freedom of the will
doesn't dodge to
winter storms.
Whispers, wishes,
love.

*

In the dark storage
of reflections, thoughts
lie clattering around,
like old heirlooms
and piles of magazines.
Rubbish that should
have been thrown away
long ago.

Among mostly
dusty memories
there is an occasional
sharp reflection,
long forgotten.
If you dig deep enough
into the mess
you can even find
a few brilliant
but faded ideas
underneath some
half-thought clutter.

Should be cleared out
and thrown away.
Only keep what is worth
thinking about again.

*

The snow crunches
underneath my shoes
and the forest listens
white of dawn.

With a little luck …

Should go home now.
Take care of my soul
and the silverware.

A lost thought.
A sleepless night.

Towards the brutal
precipice. Interrupted
at the last moment.
Where did it go?

Into the gray
mist of dawn.

The thought.

*

Like an unbridled
firestorm,
the blue rider
sweeps forward
into eternal
timelessness.
Time lives without
a beginning
or an end in an
incessant now.

An endless bridge
connects
here and there
in all directions
across miles
of light years.
Boundless space.
An infinite here.

The existence
is here and now
and constantly

on its way
to the unattainable
end of time.

The absurdity is
relentless.

*

To begin with,
I would like to ask
how the reverse side
looks, how
the other side
presents its qualities.
Is it as inviting
as the front side,
as fine, seductive
and noble?
Is it possible
that the same allure
is hidden there,
that is served to us
by the side
we have learned
to call the front.
Without insight
into its hidden
qualities,
we are fumbling
blindly.

*

Blackened
flickering images.
Burnt bridges
fade away
in the distance.
The cleansing baths
of the veils of mist
for the early
soiled.

Tirelessly
we strive towards
what we approach
all too quickly.
We don't understand
the benefit of
stilling ourselves.

*

The words,
the ones that tell
about how it was.
The spoken words
and the written ones.
The ones that create life.

Then, the precious words.
The ones that wait
to open a conversation.

Words that float
in empty space.
Nagging on in the
witching hour.
Meaningless.

The abyss opens
its blood-red mouth
and we scream
in despair our message.
One day, maybe someone
will hear us.

*

It’s impossible
to understand
that I …
that you …

We take a mayfly-walk
in sun-drenched
conversation.

Flowers and linen napkins
celebrate that
the pair of opposites
have found their
water mirrors.
It doesn't cost
to sink deep into
the mirror of the soul
before the lens
gets cloudy.

Sweeps the wing
over the wine
and your green

silver fingers.
I get up in the morning
and plant the day
beech forest green.

*

A new life.
All expectations.
It goes so fast.
Like when the snow
was new,
now long gone.